REQUIEM FOR A NUN

Requiem for a Nun

A PLAY
from the novel by
WILLIAM FAULKNER
adapted to the stage
by RUTH FORD

RANDOM HOUSE
NEW YORK

REQUIEM FOR A NUN *was first presented by The Theatre Guild with Richard Myers and Julius Fleischmann at the John Golden Theatre, New York City, on January 28, 1959, with the following cast:*

(in order of appearance)

NANCY MANNIGOE	Bertice Reading
TEMPLE	Ruth Ford
GOWAN STEVENS	Scott McKay
GAVIN STEVENS	Zachary Scott
GOVERNOR	House Jameson
PETE	Christian Flanders
MR. TUBBS	John Dorman

Directed by Tony Richardson
Original scenery and costumes by Motley
and supervised by Marvin Reiss

The action of the play takes place in the present time in the town of Jefferson, Yoknapatawpha County, Mississippi —before and after the trial of one, Nancy Mannigoe, for murder.

There are three acts.

ACT ONE

Scene 1

Courtroom. 5:30 P.M. November thirteenth.

A bell begins to toll. The curtain rises, symbolizing the rising of the prisoner in the dock. The bottom of the stage is in darkness, so that the visible scene is not only spotlighted but elevated slightly—the symbolism of the elevated tribunal of justice of which this, a county court, is only the intermediate, not the highest stage.

The defense lawyer is GAVIN STEVENS, *about fifty. He looks more like a poet than a lawyer and actually is: a bachelor, descendant of one of the pioneer Yoknapatawpha County families, Harvard and Heidelberg educated, champion not so much of truth as of justice, or of justice as he sees it, constantly involving himself, often for no pay, in affairs of equity and passion and even crime too among his people, white and Negro both, sometimes directly contrary to his office of County Attorney which he has held for years, as is the present business.*

The prisoner is standing. She is a Negress, quite black,

3

about thirty—that is, she could be almost anything between twenty and forty—with a calm impenetrable almost bemused face, not looking at anything, but looking out and up as though at some distant corner of the room, as though she were alone in it. She is—or until recently, five months ago to be exact—a domestic servant, nurse to two white children, the second of whom, an infant, she smothered in its cradle five months ago, for which act she is now on trial for her life. But she has probably done many things else, chopped cotton, cooked for working gangs—any sort of manual labor within her capacities, or rather, limitations in time and availability, since her principal reputation in the little Mississippi town where she was born is that of a tramp—a drunkard, a casual prostitute, being beaten by some man or cutting or being cut by his wife or his other sweetheart. She has probably been married, at least once. Her name—or so she calls it and would probably spell it if she could spell—is NANCY MANNIGOE.

There is a dead silence in the room while everybody watches her.

JUDGE (*Offstage, speaks through a microphone*) Have you anything to say before the sentence of the court is pronounced upon you? (NANCY *neither answers nor moves; she doesn't even seem to be listening*) That you,

4

Nancy Mannigoe, did on the thirteenth day of June, willfully and with malice aforethought kill and murder the infant child of Mr. and Mrs. Gowan Stevens in the town of Jefferson and the County of Yoknapatawpha . . . It is the sentence of this court that you be taken from hence back to the county jail of Yoknapatawpha County and there on the thirteenth day of March be hanged by the neck until you are dead. And may God have mercy on your soul.

NANCY (*Quite loud in the silence, to no one, quite calm, not moving*)   Yes, Lord. Thank you, Lord.

> (*There is a gasp, a sound, from the invisible spectators in the room, of shock at this unheard-of violation of procedure: the beginning of something which might be consternation and even uproar, in the midst of, or rather above which,* NANCY *herself does not move. From somewhere among the unseen spectators there comes the sound of a woman's voice— a moan, wail, sob perhaps. The bell tolls. The curtain descends rapidly, the lights go out. A moment of darkness. Then the curtain rises*)

Scene 2

GOWAN STEVENS' *living room. 6:00* P.M. *November thirteenth.*

The double doors in the center of the room stand open on an elevated foyer. Three steps down take you into the living room. There is a fireplace, left, with gas logs. The atmosphere of the room is smart, modern, up to date, yet the room itself has the air of another time—the high ceiling, the cornices, some of the furniture. It is all in tones of gray, with a solid red carpet.

Sound of feet, then the lights come on as if someone about to enter had pressed a wall switch, then the door opens and TEMPLE *enters, followed by* GOWAN *and* GAVIN. *She is wearing a black dress, black coat, black fur, and carries a black hat and black bag in her hands.* TEMPLE'S *air is brittle and tense, yet controlled. Her face shows nothing as she crosses to the center table and stops.* GOWAN *and* STEVENS *wear dark gray suits and overcoats, and are carrying their hats.* STEVENS *stops just inside the room.* GOWAN *drops his hat on to the chair in passing and goes on to where* TEMPLE *stands at the table, stripping off one of her gloves.*

TEMPLE (*Mimics the prisoner; her voice, harsh, reveals for the first time repressed, controlled hysteria*) Yes, God.

6

Guilty, God. Thank you, God. If that's your attitude toward being hung, what else can you expect from a judge and jury except to accommodate you?

GOWAN Stop it, Boots. Hush now. Soon as I light the fire, I'll buy a drink. (*To* STEVENS) Or maybe Gavin will do the fire while I do the butler.

TEMPLE I'll do the fire. You get the drinks. Then Uncle Gavin won't have to stay. After all, all he wants to do is say good-bye. He can almost do that in two words, if he tries hard. Then he can go home.
    (*She crosses to the hearth, kneels, and turns the gas valve, and lights the fire*)

GOWAN (*Anxiously*) Now, Boots.

TEMPLE Will you for God's sake please get me a drink?

GOWAN Sure, honey. (*He turns; to* STEVENS) Drop your coat anywhere.
    (*He exits into the dining room.* STEVENS *does not move, watching* TEMPLE *as the log takes fire*)

TEMPLE (*Still kneeling, her back to* STEVENS) If you're

7

going to stay, why don't you sit down? Or vice versa. If you're not sitting down, why don't you go? Let me be bereaved and vindicated, but at least let me do it in privacy.

(STEVENS *watches her. Then he crosses to her, taking the handkerchief from his breast pocket, stops behind her and extends the handkerchief down where she can see it. She looks at it, then up at him. Her face is quite calm*)

TEMPLE   What's that for?

STEVENS   It's all right. It's dry too. (*Still extending the handkerchief*) For tomorrow, then.

TEMPLE (*Rises quickly*)   Oh, for cinders. On the train. We're going by air; hadn't Gowan told you? We leave from the Memphis airport at midnight; we're driving up after supper. Then California tomorrow morning; maybe we'll even go on to Hawaii in the spring. No; wrong season: Canada, maybe. Lake Louise in May and June— (*She stops, listens a moment toward the dining-room doors*) So why the handkerchief? Not a threat, because you don't have anything to threaten me with, do you? And if you don't have anything to threaten me with,

I must not have anything you want, so it can't be a bribe either, can it? (*They both hear the sound from beyond the dining-room doors which indicates that* GOWAN *is approaching.* TEMPLE *lowers her voice again, rapidly*) Put it this way, then. I don't know what you want, because I don't care. Because whatever it is, you won't get it from me. (*The sound is near now—footsteps, clink of glass*) Now he'll offer you a drink, and then he'll ask you too what you want, why you followed us home. I've already answered you. No. If what you came for is to see me weep, I doubt if you'll even get that. But you certainly won't get anything else. Not from me. Do you understand that?

STEVENS I hear you.

TEMPLE Meaning, you don't believe it. (*Quicker, tenser*) I refuse to answer your question; now I'll ask you one: How much do you—(*As* GOWAN *enters, she changes what she was saying so smoothly in midsentence that anyone entering would not even realize that the pitch of her voice had altered*)—are her lawyer, she must have talked to you; even a dope fiend that murders a little baby must have what she calls some excuse for it, even a—

9

GOWAN   I said stop it, Boots. (*He carries a tray containing a pitcher of water, a bowl of ice, three empty tumblers and three whiskey glasses already filled. The bottle itself protrudes from his topcoat pocket. He approaches* TEMPLE *and offers the tray*) That's right. I'm going to have one myself. For a change. After all these years. Why not?

TEMPLE   Why not?
(*She takes one of the filled glasses.* GOWAN *offers the tray to* STEVENS, *who takes the second one. Then he sets the tray on the table and takes up the third glass*)

GOWAN   Nary a drink since we've been married. So maybe this will be a good time to start again. At least, it won't be too soon. (*To* STEVENS) Drink up. A little water behind it? (*As though not aware that he had done so, he sets his untasted glass back on the tray, splashes water from the pitcher into a tumbler, and hands the tumbler to* STEVENS *as* STEVENS *empties his glass and lowers it, taking the tumbler.* TEMPLE *has not touched hers either*) Now maybe Defense Attorney Stevens will tell us what he wants here.

STEVENS   Your wife has already told you. To say good-bye.

GOWAN Then say it. One more for the road, and where's your hat, huh?

(*He takes the tumbler from* STEVENS *and turns back to the table*)

TEMPLE (*She sets her untasted glass back on the tray*) And put ice in it this time, and maybe even a little water. But first, take Uncle Gavin's coat.

GOWAN (*Takes bottle from his pocket and makes a highball for* STEVENS *in the tumbler*) That won't be necessary. If he could raise his arm in a white courtroom to defend a murdering nigger, he can certainly bend it in nothing but a wool overcoat—at least to take a drink with the victim's mother.

TEMPLE (*She is watching, not* GOWAN *but* STEVENS, *who watches her in return, grave and soberly*) Don't forget the father too, dear.

GOWAN (*Mixing the drink*) Why should I, dear? How could I, dear? Except that the child's father is unfortunately just a man. In the eyes of the law, men are not supposed to suffer. The law is tender only of women and

children—particularly of women, particularly particular
of nigger dope fiend whores who murder white children.
(*Hands the highball to* STEVENS, *who takes it*) So why
should we expect Defense Attorney Stevens to be tender
of a man or a woman who just happened to be the parents
of the child that got murdered?

TEMPLE (*Harshly*) Will you for God's sake please get
through? Then will you for God's sake please hush?

GOWAN (*Quickly*) Sorry. (*He turns toward her, sees her
hand empty, then sees her full glass beside his own on the
tray*) No drink?

TEMPLE I don't want it. I want some milk.

GOWAN Right. Hot, of course.

TEMPLE Please.

GOWAN (*Turning*) Right. I thought of that too. I put a
pan on to heat while I was getting the drinks. (*Crossing
toward dining-room exit*) Don't let Uncle Gavin get
away until I get back. Lock the door, if you have to.

(*He exits. They don't move until the slap of the pantry door sounds*)

TEMPLE (*Rapid, hard*) How much do you know? (*Rapidly*) Don't lie to me; don't you see there's not time?

STEVENS Not time for what? Before your plane leaves tonight? Nancy has a little time yet—four months, until March, the thirteenth of March—

TEMPLE You know what I mean—her lawyer—seeing her every day—just a nigger, and you a white man—even if you needed anything to frighten her with—you could just buy it from her with a dose of cocaine or a pint of . . . (*She stops, stares at him, in a sort of amazement, despair; her voice is almost quiet*) Oh, God, oh, God. I talk about no time . . . and it's playing me button, button. She hasn't told you anything. It's me; I'm the one that's— Don't you see? It's that I cannot believe—will not believe—impossible—

STEVENS Impossible to believe that all human beings really don't—stink? No, she has told me nothing more.

TEMPLE (*Prompts*) Even if there was anything more.

STEVENS   Even if there was.

TEMPLE   Then what is it you think you know? Never mind where you got it; just tell me what you think it is.

STEVENS   There was a man here that night.

TEMPLE   (*Quick, harsh*)   So I was right. Did you frighten her, or just buy it? (*She stops; it is as if she had heard a sound presaging* GOWAN'S *return, or perhaps simply knew by instinct or from knowledge of her own house that he had had time to heat a cup of milk. Then continues, rapid and quiet*) There was no man here. You see? I told you, warned you, that you would get nothing from me. Oh, I know; you could have put me on the stand at any time, under oath; of course, your jury wouldn't have liked it—that wanton crucifixion of a bereaved mamma, but what's that in the balance with justice? I don't know why you didn't. Or maybe you still intend to—provided you can catch us before we cross the Tennessee line to-night. (*Quick, tense, hard*) All right. I'm sorry. I know better. So maybe it's just my own stinking after all that I find impossible to doubt. (*The pantry door slaps again; they both hear it*) Because I'm not even going to take

Gowan with me when I say good night— And who knows
what you might tell each other.

(She stops. GOWAN *enters, carrying a small tray bear-*
ing a glass of milk and a napkin, and comes to the
table)

GOWAN   What are you talking about now?

TEMPLE   Nothing. I was telling Uncle Gavin that he had
something of Virginia or some sort of gentleman in him
too that he must have inherited from you through your
grandfather, and that I'm going to give Bucky his
bath and supper. *(She touches the glass for heat, then*
takes it up to GOWAN*)* Thank you, dear.

GOWAN   Right, dear. *(To* STEVENS*)* You see? Not just a
napkin; the right napkin. That's how I'm trained. *(He*
stops suddenly, noticing TEMPLE, *who has done nothing*
apparently; just standing there holding the milk. But he
seems to know what is going on; to her) What's this for?

TEMPLE   I don't know. *(He moves; they kiss, not long*
but not a peck either; definitely a kiss between a man and
a woman. Then, carrying the milk, TEMPLE *crosses toward*

the hall door. To STEVENS) Good-bye then until next June. Bucky will send you and Maggie a postcard from Lake Louise.

STEVENS Where will you go then?

TEMPLE (*She goes on to the door, pauses and looks back at* STEVENS) I may even be wrong about Temple Drake's odor too; if you should happen to hear something you haven't heard yet and it's true, I may even ratify it. Maybe you can even believe that—if you can believe you are going to hear anything that you haven't heard yet.

STEVENS Do you?

TEMPLE (*After a moment*) Not from me, Uncle Gavin. If someone wants to go to heaven, who am I to stop them? Good night. Good-bye.
(*She exits, closes the door.* STEVENS, *very grave, turns back and sets his highball down on the tray*)

GOWAN Drink up. After all, I've got to eat supper and do some packing too. How about it?

STEVENS   About what? The packing, or the drink? What about you? I thought you were going to have one.

GOWAN   Oh, sure. Sure. (*Takes up the small filled glass*) Maybe you had better go on and leave us to our revenge.

STEVENS   I wish it could comfort you.

GOWAN   I wish to God it could. I wish to God that what I wanted was only revenge. An eye for an eye—were ever words emptier? Only, you have got to have lost the eye to know it.

STEVENS   Yet she still has to die.

GOWAN   Why not? Even if she would be any loss—a nigger whore, a drunkard, a dope fiend—

STEVENS   A vagabond, a tramp, hopeless until one day Mr. and Mrs. Gowan Stevens out of simple pity and humanity picked her up out of the gutter to give her one more chance— (GOWAN *stands motionless, his hand tightening slowly about the glass.* STEVENS *watches him*) And then in return for it—

GOWAN   Look, Uncle Gavin. Why don't you go for God's sake home? Or to hell, or anywhere out of here?

STEVENS   I am, in a minute. Is that why you think—why you would still say she has to die?

GOWAN   I don't. I had nothing to do with it. I wasn't even the plaintiff. I didn't even instigate the suit. My only connection with it was, I happened by chance to be the father of the child she— Who in hell ever called that a drink?

(*He dashes the whiskey, glass and all, into the ice bowl, quickly catches up one of the empty tumblers in one hand and, at the same time, tilts the whiskey bottle over it, pouring. At first he makes no sound, but at once it is obvious that he is laughing; laughter which begins normally enough, but he still pours whiskey into the glass, which in a moment now will overflow, except that* STEVENS *reaches his hand and grasps the bottle and stops it*)

STEVENS   Stop it, now. Here.

(*He takes the bottle from* GOWAN, *sets it down, takes the tumbler and tilts part of its contents into the other empty one, leaving at least a reasonable, a believable, drink, and hands it to* GOWAN. GOWAN *takes it, stopping the crazy laughter, gets hold of himself again*)

GOWAN (*Holding the glass untasted*) All those years on the wagon—and this is what I got for it: my child murdered— You see? All these years without the drink, and so I got whatever it was I was buying by not drinking, and now I've got whatever it was I was paying for and it's paid for and so I can drink again. And now I don't want the drink. So I have a laugh coming. That's triumph. Because I got a bargain even in what I didn't want. Half price: a child, and a dope fiend nigger whore on a public gallows: that's all I had to pay for immunity.

STEVENS There's no such thing.

GOWAN From the past. From my folly. My drunkenness. My cowardice, if you like—

STEVENS There's no such thing as past either.

GOWAN That is a laugh, that one. Only, not so loud, huh? to disturb the ladies—disturb Miss Drake—Miss Temple Drake. Now, Mrs. Gowan Stevens— Sure, why not cowardice. Only call it simple overtraining. You know? Gowan Stevens, trained at Virginia to drink like a gentleman, gets drunk as ten gentlemen, takes a college girl,

who knows? maybe even a virgin, cross-country by car
to another college ball game, gets drunker than twenty
gentlemen, gets lost, gets still drunker than forty gentlemen, wrecks the car, passes eighty gentlemen now, passes
completely out while the virgin is being kidnapped into
a Memphis whorehouse—(*He mumbles*)—and loved it.

STEVENS   What?

GOWAN   Sure. Call it cowardice.

STEVENS   Not the marrying her afterward, at least. What
did you—

GOWAN   Sure. Marrying her was purest Old Virginia. That
was indeed the hundred and sixty gentlemen.

STEVENS   The prisoner in the whorehouse; I didn't quite
hear—

GOWAN   (*Quickly: reaching for it*)   Where's your glass?
Dump that slop—here—

STEVENS   (*Holds glass*)   This will do. What was that you
said about held prisoner in the whorehouse?

GOWAN (*Harshly*)   That's all. You heard it.

STEVENS   You said "and loved it." (*They stare at each other*) Is that what you can never forgive her for?—for having created that moment in your life which you can never forget nor condone nor even stop thinking about, because she herself didn't even suffer, but, on the contrary, even liked it— That you had to lose not only your bachelor freedom, but your man's self-respect, to pay for something your wife didn't even regret? Is that why this poor lost doomed crazy Negro woman must die?

GOWAN (*Tensely*)   Get out of here. Go on.

STEVENS   In a minute. What else happened during that month, that time while that madman held her prisoner there in the Memphis whorehouse, that nobody but you and she know about, maybe not even you know about?
   (*Still staring at* STEVENS, *slowly and deliberately* GOWAN *sets the glass of whiskey back on the tray and takes up the bottle and swings it bottom up back over his head. The stopper is out and at once the whiskey begins to pour out of it, down his arm and sleeve and onto the floor. He does not seem to be aware of it even. His voice is tense, barely articulate*)

GOWAN   So help me, Christ . . . So help me, Christ.

(*A moment, then* STEVENS *moves, without haste, taking his hat as he passes, and goes on to the door and exits.* GOWAN *stands a moment longer with the poised bottle, now empty. Then he draws a long shuddering breath, seems to rouse, wake, sets the empty bottle back on the tray, notices his untasted whiskey glass, takes it up, a moment; then turns and throws the glass crashing into the fireplace, against the burning gas logs, and stands, his back to the audience, and draws another long shuddering breath and then draws both hands hard down his face. Then turns, looking at his wet sleeve, takes out his handkerchief and dabs at his sleeve as he comes back to the table, puts the handkerchief back in his pocket and takes the folded napkin from the small tray and wipes his sleeve with it, sees he is doing no good, tosses the crumpled napkin back on to the whiskey tray; and now, outwardly quite calm again, as though nothing had happened, he gathers the glasses back on to the tray, puts the small tray and the napkins on to it too, and takes up the tray and walks quietly toward the dining-room door as the lights begin to go down*)

Curtain

Scene 3

Living room. 10 P.M. March eleventh.

TEMPLE *enters from nursery, downstage right, closes door, on second thought opens it. She is wearing a long Chinese black brocade satin housecoat—the long loose pointed sleeves lined with red.* STEVENS *enters wearing a dark gray suit, a different one, and this time carries the top-coat and the hat, too. Apparently* TEMPLE *has already warned him to be quiet; his air, anyway, shows it.*

STEVENS   Well, here I am.

TEMPLE   Shhh. Close the nursery door.
(STEVENS *crosses to the nursery door and looks inside*)

STEVENS   You're letting Bucky sleep in the room his sister was murdered in. So this is a plant.

TEMPLE   Why not. Don't the philosophers tell us that women will strike back with any weapon, even their children?

STEVENS   Including the sleeping pill you told me on the

23

phone you gave Gowan? You came all the way back from California, almost without notice.

TEMPLE   I came all the way back from California, but I still can't seem to quit. Do you believe in coincidence?

STEVENS   I can. Yes.

TEMPLE   (*At table, takes up a folded yellow telegraph form, opens it, reads*)   Dated Jefferson, March sixth. "You have a week yet until the thirteenth. But where will you go then?" Signed Gavin.
   (*She folds the paper back into its old creases, folds it still again.* STEVENS *watches her*)

STEVENS   Well? This is the eleventh. Is that the coincidence?

TEMPLE   No. This is. (*Sits in front of the fire—clutching the folded paper*) It was that very afternoon—the sixth. We were on the beach, Bucky and I. I was reading, and he was—oh, talking mostly, you know—"Is California far from Jefferson, Mamma?" and I say, "Yes, darling" —you know: still reading or trying to, and he says, "How

24

long will we stay in California, Mamma?" and I say, "Until we get tired of it," and he says, "Will we stay here until they hang Nancy, Mamma?" I say, "Yes, darling," and then he drops it right in my lap, right out of the mouths of babes and sucklings. "Where will we go then, Mamma?" So I went back to the hotel and got reservations and here we are and I got Gowan—I hope—safely in bed with a barbital, and telephoned you. Well?

STEVENS   Well what?

TEMPLE   All right. Let's for God's sake stop. (*Goes to a chair*) Now that I'm here, no matter who's responsible for it, what do you want? A drink? Will you drink? At least, put your coat and hat down. (STEVENS *lays his hat and coat on a chair.* TEMPLE *sits down.* STEVENS *takes a chair opposite*) So Nancy must be saved. Apparently I know something I haven't told yet, or maybe you know something I haven't told yet. What do you think you know? (*Quickly; he says nothing*) All right. What do you know?

STEVENS   Nothing. I don't want to know it. All I—

TEMPLE   All right. Why do you think there is something I haven't told yet?

STEVENS   You came back. All the way from California.

TEMPLE   Not enough. Try again.

STEVENS   You were there. (*With her face averted,* TEMPLE *reaches her hand to the table, fumbles until she finds the cigarette box, takes a cigarette*) At the trial. Every day. All day, from the time court opened—

TEMPLE   (*Still not looking at him, supremely casual*) The bereaved mother—

STEVENS   Yes, the bereaved mother—

TEMPLE   —herself watching the accomplishment of her revenge; the tigress over the body of her slain cub—

STEVENS   —who should have been too immersed in grief to have thought of revenge—to have borne the very sight of her child's murderer . . .

TEMPLE   (*Not looking at him*)   Methinks she doth protest too much?

   (STEVENS *doesn't answer. He snaps the lighter on,*

26

*lights her cigarette, puts the lighter back on the table.
Leaning,* STEVENS *pushes the ash tray along the table
until she can reach it. Now she looks at him*)

TEMPLE Thanks. Now let grandmamma teach you how to
suck an egg. It doesn't matter what I know, what you
think I know, what might have happened. Because we
won't even need it. All we need is an affidavit. That she is
crazy. Has been for years.

STEVENS I thought of that too. Only it's too late. That
should have been done about five months ago. She has
been convicted and sentenced. In the eyes of the law, she
is already dead. In the eyes of the law, Nancy Mannigoe
doesn't even exist.

TEMPLE (*Smoking*) Yes? (*She sits back in the chair,
smoking rapidly, looking at* STEVENS. *Her voice is gentle,
patient, only a little too rapid, like the smoking*) Now
try to listen. Really try. I am the affidavit; what else are
we doing here at ten o'clock at night barely a day from
her execution? What else did I come all the way back
from California for? All we need now is to decide just
how much of what to put in the affidavit. Do try; maybe
you had better have a drink after all.

STEVENS   Later, maybe. I'm dizzy enough right now with just perjury and contempt of court.

TEMPLE   What perjury?

STEVENS   After my client is not only convicted but sentenced, I turn up with the prosecution's chief witness offering evidence to set the whole trial aside—

TEMPLE   Tell them I forgot this. Or tell them I changed my mind. Tell them the district attorney bribed me to keep my mouth shut—

STEVENS   (*Peremptory yet quiet*)   Temple.
        (*She puffs rapidly at the cigarette, removes it from her mouth*)

TEMPLE   Or better still—a woman whose child was smothered in its crib, wanting vengeance, capable of anything to get the vengeance; then when she has it, realizing she can't go through with it, can't sacrifice a human life for it, even a nigger whore's?

STEVENS   Stop it. One at a time. At least, let's talk about the same thing. Then you really don't want her to die.

TEMPLE   Oh, for God's sake, didn't I just say so?

STEVENS   Then Temple Drake will have to save her.

TEMPLE   Mrs. Gowan Stevens will.

STEVENS   Temple Drake. (*She stares at him, smoking, deliberately now. Deliberately she removes the cigarette and, still watching him, reaches and snubs it out in the ash tray*) All right. We produce a sworn affidavit that Nancy was crazy when she committed the crime. Based on what?

TEMPLE   —What?

STEVENS   Based on what proof?
          (*She stares at him*)

TEMPLE   Proof?

STEVENS   What will be in the affidavit? What are we going to affirm now that for some reason we didn't see fit to bring up or anyway didn't bring up until after she—

29

TEMPLE How do I know? You're the lawyer. What do such affidavits need to have in them, to make them work, make them sure to work? (*Her voice ceases. She stares at him, while he continues to look steadily back at her, saying nothing, just looking at her, until at last she draws a loud harsh breath; her voice is harsh too*) What do you want then? What more do you want?

STEVENS Temple Drake.

TEMPLE (*Quick, harsh, immediate*) No. Mrs. Gowan Stevens.

STEVENS (*Implacable and calm*) Temple Drake. The truth.

TEMPLE Truth? We're trying to save a condemned murderess whose lawyer has already admitted that he has failed. What has truth got to do with that? (*Rapid, harsh*) Can't you get it through your head that I will do anything, *anything?*

STEVENS Except one. Which is all, everything. We're not concerned with death. That's nothing. What we are trying to deal with now is injustice. Only truth can cope with that. Or love.

TEMPLE (*Harshly*)   Love. Oh, God. Love.

STEVENS   Call it pity then. Or courage. Or honesty, or a simple desire for the right to sleep at night.

TEMPLE   You prate of sleep, to me, who learned years ago how not even to realize any more that I didn't mind not sleeping at night? If her dying is nothing, what in God's name do you want?

STEVENS   I told you. Truth.

TEMPLE   And I told you that truth has nothing to do with this. When you go before the supreme court what you will need will be facts, sworn documents.

STEVENS   We're not going to the supreme court. (*She stares at him*) We're going to the Governor. Tonight.

TEMPLE   The Governor?

STEVENS   Perhaps he won't save her either. He probably won't.

TEMPLE   Then why ask him? Why?

STEVENS   I've told you. Truth.

TEMPLE   (*In quiet amazement*)   For no more than that. For no better reason than that. Just to get it told, breathed aloud, into words, sound. Just to be heard by someone, anyone, any stranger none of whose business it is, simply because he is capable of hearing it, comprehending it. Why blink your own rhetoric? Why don't you go on and tell me it's for the good of my soul—if I have one?

STEVENS   I did. I said, so you can sleep at night.

TEMPLE   And I told you I forgot years ago even what it was to miss the sleep. (*She stares at him. He doesn't answer, looking at her. She turns her head and looks toward the nursery door*) So it was a plant, after all; I just didn't seem to know for who. I threw my remaining child at you. Now you threw him back.

STEVENS   But I didn't wake him.

TEMPLE   Then I've got you, lawyer. What would be better for his peace and sleep than to hang his sister's murderer?

STEVENS   No matter by what means, in what lie?

TEMPLE   Nor whose.

STEVENS   Yet you came back.

TEMPLE   Mrs. Gowan Stevens did.

STEVENS   Temple Drake did. Mrs. Gowan Stevens is not even fighting in this class. This is Temple Drake's.

TEMPLE   Temple Drake is dead.

STEVENS   The past is never dead. It's not even past.

TEMPLE   Listen. How much do you know?

STEVENS   Nothing.

TEMPLE   Swear.

STEVENS   Would you believe me?

TEMPLE   No. But swear anyway.

STEVENS All right. I swear.

TEMPLE All right. How much do you *think* you know?

STEVENS There was a man here that night.

TEMPLE (*Quickly*) Gowan.

STEVENS Let's agree that this is for your life too. So nobody but a fool would expect you to fight by Queensberry
rules. But only a fool would believe you foolish enough
to mistake a straw for a cudgel. Gowan wasn't here then.
He and Bucky left at six o'clock that morning for New
Orleans to go fishing. It was Gowan himself who gave
you away—something he said to me without knowing
he was doing it, which showed who planned that trip,
to get not only Gowan, but Bucky too out of this house.
I'm surprised you didn't send Nancy away too— (*He
stops, obviously reacts to something he sees in* TEMPLE'S
face) Why, you did. You did try, and she refused. Yes.
There was a man here that night.

TEMPLE Prove it.

34

STEVENS   I can't. Don't I keep on saying that Nancy has refused to tell me anything about that night?

TEMPLE   Now listen to me. (*She stands, tense, rigid, facing him, staring at him*) Listen carefully, because I don't intend to say this again. Temple Drake is dead. Temple Drake will have been dead years longer than Nancy Mannigoe will ever be. If there is anything—anything at all—that Mrs. Gowan Stevens can sign or swear to or lie to, to save Nancy Mannigoe, I will do it. But if all Nancy Mannigoe has left to save her is Temple Drake, then God help Nancy Mannigoe. Now get out of here. (*She stares at him; another moment. Then he rises, still watching her; she stares steadily and implacably back. Then he moves*) Good night.

STEVENS   Good night.
(*He goes back to the chair, takes up his coat and hat, then goes on to the hall door, and exits.* TEMPLE *stands watching the door. When* STEVENS *is gone,* GOWAN *appears quietly in the door, in his shirt sleeves, tieless, his collar open. He watches* TEMPLE *and she stands a moment longer. Then she makes a gesture something like* GOWAN'S *in Scene 2, except that she merely presses her hands hard against her*

cheeks, stands a moment, then drops her hands and crosses purposefully to the telephone, GOWAN *still watching her, and lifts receiver*)

TEMPLE (*Into the phone*) Three-two-nine, please. (*She does not see* GOWAN *yet. He approaches her, carrying something in his closed hand. He is right behind her when the phone answers*) Hello. Maggie? This is Temple. When Uncle Gavin—

(GOWAN *reaches roughly past her, grasps her hand holding the receiver and claps the receiver back on the stand, cutting off the connection; at the same time he flips the capsule from his other hand onto the table*)

GOWAN There's your pill too. Why don't you tell me about the man that Gavin says was here that night? Come on. You won't even have to think hard. Just tell me he was an uncle of Bucky's that you just forgot to tell me about.

TEMPLE Would you believe me if I said there wasn't one?

GOWAN Sure I would. Anything you say. I always have. That's what has sunk us. I even believed right up until tonight that it was me that planned that fishing trip.

Everybody but me knew better, but that was all right, nobody needed to be fooled but me and I was already on my back when I came in. Thanks though. But I can still see, even if I don't know until years afterward what I was looking at. But try the truth maybe; there surely must be something you can tell me that I won't believe. Maybe Gavin was right and his business wasn't with my wife, but with Temple Drake. Maybe it was Bucky's papa, huh, just dropped in on the way through town—

TEMPLE Gowan, hush. (*He stops talking, looking at her*) Why can't you just hush?
(*She indicates the sleeping child*)

GOWAN Don't worry, you were the one who seems to worry about waking him. I'm not going to make that much noise. I'm not going to hit you. I never hit a woman in my life, not even a whore, not even a Memphis whore, an ex-Memphis whore— Jesus, they say there are two women every man is entitled to hit once; his wife, and his whore. And just look at me; I can hit both of mine at one time, with one swing, one lick— Do you want a drink?

TEMPLE No. I don't want one.

GOWAN   Come on. I'll fix you one.

TEMPLE   I don't want one.

GOWAN   (*Produces pack of cigarettes from his trouser pocket and offers one*)   Then have a cigarette, then. For Christ's sake, do something. Don't just stand there. (TEMPLE *takes the cigarette. He produces a lighter from the same pocket and snaps it on*) Here. (*She accepts the light. He puts the lighter back into his pocket, drops the pack of cigarettes on to the table*) Okay, I've stopped. Now we can start even. If we just could, of course. But with all these big-wheel international truths knocking around here tonight, it's no wonder you and I can't get together on a little petty fact like how a man's wife just treating herself to a little extracurricular poontang should cause the murder of their child—

TEMPLE   That's right. Go ahead. Then maybe we can stop.

GOWAN   Because you really do believe it, don't you? That there really is some price, some point where you can stop paying, some last nickel you've got in the world that they won't ask of you, that you won't have to pay for just one mistake—mistake—mistake? Jesus, let's laugh. Come on, laugh. Don't just stand there—

TEMPLE (*Sharply*) Gowan! Stop it!

GOWAN That's right. Slap me, try that. Hit me. Then maybe I will hit you back and then you can start forgiving me for a change. You know, for the whole thing; getting drunk that day, not because I wanted to get drunk, but because I was afraid, afraid that I, the big wheel, Joe College himself, president of his frat at Charlottesville, who could even call the madams of New York City cathouses by their first names, couldn't handle a little Mississippi country girl who had never been away from home until she entered the freshman class at the State University —had to get drunk to have enough courage to persuade you to slip out of that damned baseball excursion train.

TEMPLE Did you twist my arm?

GOWAN What?

TEMPLE You didn't have to persuade— All you had to do was suggest.

39

GOWAN Will you shut up? Will you? Let me have a good whine while I'm at it. Tell me what you probably think I've been telling myself all these years: how, if it hadn't been for you, I might have married a good girl—a decent girl that never heard of hot pants until her husband taught her— (*He stops, drags his hands down his face again as in Scene 2*) God, we must have loved each other once. We must have. Can't you remember.

TEMPLE Yes.

GOWAN Yes what?

TEMPLE Loved one another once. We must have.

GOWAN Can't you remember! Can't you? (*She doesn't answer*) Come here.

TEMPLE (*Not moving*) No.

GOWAN All right. If you want it this way, you can have it. You're not going to use that telephone. There was a man here that night—

40

TEMPLE   No.

GOWAN   (*Pays no attention*)   —since Uncle Gavin knows
it, I suppose everybody else in Jefferson does too—except
me of course. Though I still don't see how that brought
about the murder of a six-months-old baby. Maybe Nancy
caught you laying him, and killed Dee Dee in spite or
excitement or something. Or maybe the excitement wasn't
Nancy's; that in your hurry you forgot to move Dee Dee
out of the bed, and in the general thrashing around—
You see? You see what I am capable of? I don't even have
to half try . . .

TEMPLE   No.

GOWAN   No what? Go on. Say it. There was no man here.
(TEMPLE *says nothing*) Go on. Can't you say it? (TEMPLE
says nothing) All right then. At least you didn't tell
Gavin what happened here that night. So I don't want to
know what happened. And so nobody else shall. Not ever.
You're not going to call Uncle Gavin and agree to go tell
the Governor or anybody else anything. You said it yourself: if all Nancy Mannigoe's got to save her is Temple
Drake, then God help Nancy Mannigoe. Okay?

TEMPLE No.

GOWAN Oh yes. You see, I'm even giving you one more chance. If there is any reason for grief and suffering, it's so that you will learn at least not to make the same mistake again, and to have consideration for the mistakes that other people make, and to believe that they are going to try not to make the same ones any more. But I still believe that there is some drop of blood you won't have to pay for what you did and can't recall. So you are not going to touch that telephone. Because if you go, I'm gone. (*Quickly*) Wait. You could have quit at any time. You still can. But if you pick up that telephone and call Uncle Gavin, it will be too late. It will be me that's gone. Okay? (*She doesn't answer*) Say yes, Temple.

TEMPLE I can't.

GOWAN Say yes, Temple. We loved each other once. Didn't we?

TEMPLE We must have.

GOWAN Then say it. You said it once.

TEMPLE   We loved each other once.

GOWAN   Then prove it. If she must die, let her. If something happened here that night that would save her and she won't tell it, then who are you—

TEMPLE   I can't.

GOWAN   Temple— (*They watch each other for a moment. Then* TEMPLE *turns toward the telephone.* GOWAN *moves faster, reaches it first, and puts his hand on the receiver*) Remember.

TEMPLE   Please move your hand, Gowan. (*They watch each other. Then he removes his hand.* TEMPLE *takes the receiver. Into the phone*) Three-two-nine, please . . .

Curtain

ACT TWO

ACT TWO

Scene 1

Office of the Governor of the State. 2:00 A.M. March twelfth.

The whole bottom of the stage is in darkness, as in Act One, Scene 1, so that the visible scene has the effect of being held in the beam of a spotlight; the elevated foyer carrying still further the symbolism of the still higher, the last, the ultimate seat of judgment. It has now become the office of the Governor of the Commonwealth. The center doors are now covered with black velvet. Hanging on this is a large eagle, the blind scales of justice, a device in Latin perhaps, against a flag. There is a massive flat-topped desk, bare except for an ash tray and a cigarette box. Beyond it there is a black, high-backed heavy chair like a throne. Hanging high above is the emblem, official badge, of the State, sovereignty (a mythical one, since this is rather the State of which Yoknapatawpha County is a unit). There are two other chairs in front of the desk, turned slightly to face each other.

The GOVERNOR *stands in front of the high chair, between*

it and the desk, beneath the emblem on the wall. He is sym-
bolic too: no known person, neither old nor young; he might
be someone's idea not of God but of Gabriel, perhaps, the
Gabriel not before the Crucifixion but after it. He has ob-
viously just been routed out of bed or at least out of his
study or dressing room; he wears a dressing gown, though
there is a collar and tie beneath it, and his hair is neatly
combed.

It is obvious that the arrival of someone is imminent.
After a few seconds GOWAN *enters hurriedly from the left,*
nervous and expectant. There is a moment of pantomime
and the GOVERNOR *sends him off in the direction he came*
from. This has just barely been accomplished when STEVENS
enters from the right. He exchanges a greeting with the
GOVERNOR *and calls* TEMPLE *on.* TEMPLE *enters wearing*
the same black dress and coat.

STEVENS   Good morning, Henry. Here we are.

GOVERNOR   Yes. Sit down. (*As* TEMPLE *sits down*) Does
Mrs. Stevens smoke?

STEVENS   Yes. Thank you.
    (*The* GOVERNOR *extends the cigarette box to* TEMPLE.
    STEVENS *lights* TEMPLE'S *cigarette*)

48

TEMPLE   Thanks.

> (*The* GOVERNOR *sits down in the tall chair behind the desk, his hands resting on the desk before him.* STEVENS *sits down in the other chair across from* TEMPLE)

GOVERNOR   What has Mrs. Gowan Stevens to tell me?

TEMPLE   Not Mrs. Gowan Stevens: Temple Drake.

GOVERNOR   What has Temple Drake to tell me then?

TEMPLE   How much will I have to tell? I mean, how much of it that you don't already know?

GOVERNOR   Tell me about Nancy—Mannihoe, Mannikoe —how does she spell it?

TEMPLE   She doesn't. She can't. She can't read or write either.

GOVERNOR   Why not start by telling me about her?

TEMPLE   She was a dope fiend whore that my husband and

I took out of the gutter to nurse our children. She murdered one of them and is to be hung tomorrow morning.
We—her lawyer and I—have come to ask you to save
her.

GOVERNOR   Yes. I know all that. Why?

TEMPLE   Because I have forgiven her. (*The* GOVERNOR
watches her, he and STEVENS *both do, waiting. She stares
back at the* GOVERNOR *steadily, not defiant: just alert*)
Because she was crazy. (*The* GOVERNOR *watches her: she
stares back, puffing rapidly at the cigarette*) All right.
You don't mean why I am asking you to save her, but why
I hired a whore and a tramp and a dope fiend to nurse
our children. To give her another chance—a human being
too—

STEVENS   No, Temple, not for that reason.

TEMPLE   (*Rapidly, with a sort of despair*)   Why can't I
stop lying?

GOVERNOR   Yes. Go on.

TEMPLE (*She puffs rapidly at the cigarette, leans and crushes
it out in the ash tray and sits erect again. She speaks in a*

hard rapid brittle emotionless voice) Whore, dope fiend;
hopeless, already damned before she was ever born, whose
only reason for living was to get the chance to die on the
gallows. Who made her debut into public life lying in
the gutter with a white man trying to kick her teeth down
her throat. You remember, Gavin: what was his name?
the pillar of the church. Well, this Monday morning and
still drunk, Nancy comes up while he is unlocking the
front door of the bank and fifty people standing at his
back to get in, and Nancy comes into the crowd and right
up to him and says, "Where's my two dollars, white
man?" and he turned and struck her, knocked her across
the pavement into the gutter, stomping and kicking at
her face or anyway her voice which was still saying,
"Where's my two dollars, white man? It was two dollars
more than two weeks ago and you done been back twice
since"— (*She stops speaking, presses both hands to her
face for an instant, then removes them*) So now I've got
to tell all of it. Because that was just Nancy Mannigoe.
Temple Drake was in more than just a two-dollar Satur-
day-night house. (*She leans forward and starts to take up
the crushed cigarette from the ash tray.* STEVENS *picks up
the pack from the desk and prepares to offer it to her. She
withdraws her hand from the crushed cigarette and sits
back. To the proffered cigarette in* STEVENS' *hand*) No,

thanks. So how much will I have to tell about Temple Drake that I never thought that anything on earth, least of all the murder of my child, would ever make me tell? You know: how much will I have to tell, to make it good and painful of course, but quick too, so that you can revoke or commute the sentence or whatever you do to it, and we can all go back home to sleep or at least to bed?

STEVENS Tell him, then.

TEMPLE He hasn't answered my question yet. (*To the* GOVERNOR) Don't just say "everything." I've already heard that.

GOVERNOR I know who Temple Drake was: the young woman student at the University some years ago who left the school one morning on a special train of students to attend a baseball game at another college, and disappeared from the train somewhere during its run, and vanished, nobody knew where, until she reappeared six weeks later as a witness in a murder trial in Jefferson.

STEVENS Wait. Let me play too. She got off the train at the instigation of a young man, Gowan Stevens, my nephew, who met the train at an intermediate stop, the plan being to drive on to the ball game in his car, except that he was drunk at the time and got drunker, and wrecked the car and stranded both of them at the moon- shiner's house where the murder happened, and from which the murderer kidnapped her and carried her to Memphis, to hold her until he would need his alibi. It was Gowan who knew the moonshiner and insisted on going there.

TEMPLE (*To* STEVENS, *quick and harsh*) And married me for it. Does he have to pay for it twice? It wasn't really worth paying for once, was it?

GOVERNOR How much was it worth?

TEMPLE Was what worth?

GOVERNOR His marrying you.

TEMPLE You mean to him, of course. Less than he paid for it.

GOVERNOR Is that what he thinks too? (*They stare at one*

53

another, TEMPLE *alert, quite watchful, though rather impatient than anything else*) You're going to tell me something that he doesn't know, else you would have brought him with you. Is that right?

TEMPLE   Yes.

GOVERNOR   Would you tell it if he were here?
    (TEMPLE *is staring at the* GOVERNOR. *Unnoticed by her,* STEVENS *makes a faint movement. The* GOVERNOR *stops him with a slight motion of one hand which also* TEMPLE *does not notice*)

TEMPLE   He's not. He's at home.

GOVERNOR   But suppose he was, now that you have got to say it. Would you still say it?

TEMPLE   Yes. Now will you please let me tell it? How can I, if you and Gavin won't hush and let me? I saw the murder, and the murderer, they called him Popeye, took me to Memphis, and I know that, I had two legs and I could see, and I could have simply screamed up the main street of any of the little towns we passed, and stopped a car which would have carried me back to school or, for that matter, right on back home. But not me, not Temple. I choose the murderer—

STEVENS (*To the* GOVERNOR) He was a psychopath: a little black thing, like a neat and only slightly deformed cockroach: sexually incapable. But then, she will tell you that too.

TEMPLE (*With bitter sarcasm*) Dear Uncle Gavin.

STEVENS (*To the* GOVERNOR) Oh yes, that too, her bad luck too: to plump for a thing which didn't even have sex for his weakness, but just murder—

TEMPLE I was carried to Memphis and shut up in that sporting house like a ten-year-old bride in a Spanish convent, with the madam herself more eagle-eyed than any mamma—and a Negro maid to guard the door while the madam would be out, to wherever she would go, wherever the madams of cathouses go on their afternoons out, which would not be so bad because the maid would unlock the door and come inside and we could talk. (*She falters, pauses for less than a second; then quickly*) He brought

55

me perfume by the quart, the wrong kind of course, and a fur coat, and snazzy underwear and negligees. Because he wanted me to be contented, you see; and not only contented, he didn't even mind if I was happy too. And so at last we have come to it, because now I have got to tell you this too to give you a valid reason why I waked you up at two in the morning to ask you to save a murderess. Because I still had the two arms and legs and eyes; I could have climbed down the rainspout at any time, the only difference being that I didn't. I was never allowed to leave my room. I wasn't even permitted to meet the other girls in my own house, not even to sit with them after work and listen to the shop talk while they counted their chips or blisters or whatever they would do sitting on one another's beds in the elected dormitory— (*She pauses again, continues in a sort of surprise, amazement*) Yes, it was like the dormitory at school: the smell: of women, all busy thinking not about men but just man: only a little stronger, sitting on the temporarily idle beds discussing the exigencies of their trade. But not me, not Temple: shut up in that room twenty-four hours a day, with nothing to do but hold fashion shows in the fur coat and the flashy pants, with nothing to see it but a two-foot mirror and a Negro maid; hanging bone dry and safe in the middle of sin and pleasure like being suspended twenty

fathoms deep in an ocean diving bell. Because he wanted her to be contented, you see. But Temple didn't want to be just contented. So she had to do what us sporting girls call fall in love.

STEVENS   That's right.

TEMPLE   (*Quickly, to* STEVENS)   Hush.

STEVENS   (*To the* GOVERNOR)   Popeye brought the man there himself. He—the young man—

TEMPLE   Gavin! No, I tell you!

STEVENS   (*To the* GOVERNOR)   He was known in his own circles as Red, Alabama Red. He was the bouncer at the nightclub on the outskirts of town, which Popeye owned.

GOVERNOR   I see. This—Popeye—

STEVENS   He was a hybrid, impotent. He should have been crushed somehow under a vast and mindless boot, like a spider. He didn't sell her. He was a purist: he did not even murder for base profit. It was not even for simple lust. He was a gourmet, a sybarite.

57

GOVERNOR   I don't think I understand.

STEVENS   Try to.

TEMPLE   Or don't try to. Just let it go. Just for God's sake let it go. I met the man, how doesn't matter, and I fell what I called in love with him and what it was or what I called it doesn't matter either because all that matters is that I wrote the letters—

GOVERNOR   I see. Is this the part that your husband doesn't know?

TEMPLE (*To the* GOVERNOR)   And what does that matter either? What can another face or two or name or two matter, since he knows that I lived for six weeks in a brothel? I'm trying to tell it, enough of it. Can't you see that? But make him, for God's sake, let me alone.

GOVERNOR (*To* STEVENS, *watching* TEMPLE)   No more, Gavin. (*To* TEMPLE) So you fell in love.

TEMPLE   Thank you for that. I mean, the "love." Except that I didn't even fall, I was already there. So I wrote the

58

letters. I would write one each time . . . afterward, after they—he left.

GOVERNOR What? What's that? You said, after *they* left. (*They look at one another.* TEMPLE *doesn't answer. To* STEVENS, *though still watching* TEMPLE) Am I being told that this . . . Popeye would be there in the room too?

STEVENS Yes. He was sexually incapable. That was why he brought Red. You see now what I meant by connoisseur and gourmet.

GOVERNOR And what you meant by the boot too. (*To* TEMPLE) Yes. Go on. The letters.

TEMPLE The letters. They were good letters. I mean— good ones. Better than you would expect from an amateur. I mean, you would have wondered how I could have learnt the—right words. What I'm trying to say is, they were the kind of letters that if you'd written them to a man, you would rather your husband didn't see them, no matter what he thought about your past. And that's all.

STEVENS (*To* TEMPLE) Yes, that's all. But you've got to tell him why it's all.

TEMPLE I thought I had. The man I wrote them to died, and I married another man and reformed, or thought I had. I even thought I had forgotten about the letters. You've certainly heard of blackmail. The letters turned up again, of course. And, of course, being Temple Drake, the first way to buy them back that Temple Drake thought of was to produce the material for another set of them. Then I found out that I not only hadn't forgot about the letters, I hadn't even reformed—

GOVERNOR The young man Red died, you said.

TEMPLE Yes— Died, shot from a car while he was slipping up the alley behind the house, climbing up the drainpipe to see me—the one time, the only time when we thought we had dodged, fooled Popeye, could be alone together, just the two of us, after all the—other ones. If love can mean anything, except the newness, the learning, the peace, the privacy: no shame: not even conscious that you are naked because you are just using the nakedness because that's a part of it; then he was killed, shot down right in the middle of thinking about me, when in just

60

one more minute he would have been in the room with me, when all of him except just his body was already in the room with me; and then it was all over as though it had never happened.

STEVENS   Then Popeye's trial for murder—Temple lied for him and he was acquitted.

TEMPLE   And I didn't care, not about anything any more, and then the year in Europe, and I still didn't care.

STEVENS   Then Gowan went to Paris that winter and they were married.

TEMPLE   (*Rapidly now, tense, erect, her hands gripped again into fists on her lap*)   I just wanted the two of us to kneel down and say "We have sinned, forgive us." And then maybe there would be the love this time—the peace, the quiet, the no shame that I . . . missed that other time— (*Falters again, then rapidly again, glib and succinct*) Love, but more than love too: not depending on just love to hold two people together, but tragedy, suffering: that there was something even better than tragedy to hold two people together: forgiveness. Only that seemed to be wrong. Only maybe it wasn't the forgiveness that was wrong, but the gratitude; and maybe the only thing worse than having to give gratitude all the time, is having to accept it—

STEVENS Which is exactly backward. What was wrong wasn't—

GOVERNOR Gavin.

STEVENS —Temple's good name. It wasn't even her husband's conscience. It was his vanity. So the forgiving wasn't enough for him. Because after about a year, he began to doubt the paternity of their child.

TEMPLE Oh God. Oh God.

GOVERNOR (*To* TEMPLE) Yes. Tell me.

TEMPLE I'm trying to. Let's see, we'd got back to Jefferson, back home. You know; face it: the disgrace: the shame, face it down, good and down forever. The Gowan Stevenses, young, popular: a new house on the right street, a country club, a pew in the right church.

STEVENS   Then the son and heir came; and now we are
back to Nancy: nurse: guide: catalyst, glue, whatever you
want to call it, holding the whole lot of them together:
the only animal in Jefferson that spoke Temple Drake's
language.

TEMPLE   Oh yes, I'm going to tell that too. A confidante.
Two sisters in sin swapping trade or anyway avocational
secrets over Coca-Colas in the quiet kitchen. Somebody
to talk to, as we all seem to need. Which is all that people
really want, really need. I mean, to behave themselves,
keep out of one another's hair.

STEVENS   Now she couldn't escape; she had waited too
long. But it was worse than that. It was as though she
realized for the first time that you—everyone—must, or
anyway may have to, pay for your past. But she found a
hope: which was the child's own tender and defenseless
innocence: that God—if there was one—would protect
the child—not her: that when He said "Suffer little children to come unto Me" He meant exactly that: He meant
suffer; that the adults, the fathers, the old in and capable
of sin, must be ready and willing—nay, eager—to suffer
at any time, that the little children shall come unto Him
unanguished, unterrified, undefiled. Do you accept that?

GOVERNOR Go on.

STEVENS So at least she had ease. Not hope: ease. It was precarious of course, but she could walk a tightrope too. It was as though she had struck an armistice with God. She had not tried to cheat.

GOVERNOR Go on.

STEVENS So you can take your choice about the second child. Perhaps she was too busy between the three of them to be careful enough: between the three of them: the doom, the fate, the past; the bargain with God; the forgiveness and the gratitude. She just didn't have time to be careful enough. Anyway, she was pregnant again, and she probably knew fifteen months before the murder of her child that this was the end. (*The lights begin to dim*) She had merely been wondering for fifteen months what form the doom would take. Now tell it.

> (*As the lights begin to dim the double doors close and* TEMPLE *slowly walks down the center stairs. During the moment of blackout she takes off her coat, throws it across the back of the chair, picks up the phone and, as the lights come on, we are back in the living room*)

Scene 2

Interior, living room. 9:30 P.M. June thirteenth ante.
When the lights go up, PETE *is pacing back and forth.*
He is about twenty-five. He does not look like a criminal.
That is, he is not a standardized recognizable criminal or
gangster type, quite. He looks almost like the general con-
ception of a college man, or a successful young automobile
or appliance salesman. His clothes are ordinary, neither flashy
nor sharp, simply what everybody wears. But there is a defi-
nite "untamed" air to him. He is handsome, attractive to
women, not at all unpredictable because you—or they—
know exactly what he will do, you just hope he won't do it
this time. He has a hard ruthless quality, not immoral but
unmoral.

He wears a light-weight summer suit, his hat is shoved
onto the back of his head so that, engaged as he is at present,
he looks exactly like a youthful city detective in a tough
moving picture.

A table, center, bears TEMPLE'S *hat, gloves and bag, also*
a bag such as is associated with infants; two bags, obviously
TEMPLE'S, *are packed and closed and sit on the floor beside*
the table. The whole room indicates TEMPLE'S *imminent*
departure, and that something has been vainly yet savagely
and completely, perhaps even frantically, searched for.

65

TEMPLE *is talking on the phone: "Yes—uh-huh—I see—uh-huh—thank you very much." She hangs up.*

PETE Well?

TEMPLE No. The people where she lives say they haven't seen her since she left to come to work this morning.

PETE I could have told you that. (*He glances at his wrist watch*) We've still got time. Where does she live?

TEMPLE (*At the table*) And then what? Hold a lighted cigarette against the sole of her foot?

PETE It's two thousand dollars. Besides the jewelry. What do you suggest then? Call the cops?

TEMPLE No. You won't have to run. I'm giving you an out.

PETE An out?

TEMPLE No dough, no snatch. Isn't that how you would say it?

66

PETE   Maybe I don't get you.

TEMPLE   You can quit now. Clear out. Leave. Then all you'll have to do is, wait till my husband gets back, and start over.

PETE   Maybe I still don't get you.

TEMPLE   You've still got the letters, haven't you?

PETE   Oh, the letters. (*He reaches inside his coat, takes out the packet of letters and tosses it to* TEMPLE, *who is standing by the fireplace*) There you are.

TEMPLE   I told you two days ago I didn't want them.

PETE   Sure. That was two days ago. (TEMPLE *strikes a match, stands motionless, the packet of letters in one hand, the burning match in the other. Then she turns her head and looks back at him. For another moment they watch each other*) Go ahead. Burn them. The other time I gave them to you, you turned them down so you could always change your mind and back out. Burn them. (*They watch each other for another moment. Then she turns her head*

and stands now, her face averted, the match still burning.
PETE *watches her for another moment*) Then put that
junk down and come here. (*She blows out the match, puts
the packet of letters on the mantelpiece as she passes it,
and crosses to* PETE, *who has not moved. At this moment,*
NANCY'S *shadow appears behind the closed doors. Neither
of them sees her.* PETE *puts his arms around* TEMPLE) I
offered you an out too. (*He draws her closer*) Baby.

TEMPLE Don't call me that.

PETE (*Tightens his arms, caressing and savage too*) Red
did. I'm as good a man as my brother was. Ain't I?
   (*They kiss.* NANCY *moves quietly through the door
and stops just inside the room, watching them. She
now wears the standardized department-store maid-
servant's uniform, but without cap or apron, beneath
a light-weight open topcoat; on her head is a battered
almost shapeless felt hat which must have once be-
longed to a man.* TEMPLE *feels her presence and
breaks the kiss.* PETE *sees* NANCY *across* TEMPLE'S
shoulder, and reacts. TEMPLE *reacts to him, turns
quickly and sees* NANCY *too.* NANCY *comes on into
the room*)

TEMPLE (*To* NANCY) What are you doing here?

NANCY I brought my foot. So he can hold that cigarette against it.

TEMPLE So you're not just a thief: you're a spy too.

PETE Maybe she's not a thief either. Maybe she brought it back. (*They watch* NANCY, *who doesn't answer*) Or maybe she didn't. Maybe we had better use that cigarette. How about it? Is that what you came back for, sure enough?

TEMPLE (*To* PETE) Hush. Take the bags and go on to the car.

PETE (*Meaningly*) I'll wait for you. There may be a little something I can do here, after all.

TEMPLE Go on, I tell you! Let's for God's sake get away from here.

(PETE *watches* NANCY *for a moment longer, who stands facing them but not looking at anything, motionless, almost bemused, her face sad, brooding and*

69

inscrutable. Then PETE *turns, goes to the mantel, takes up the packet of letters, pauses, then drops the letters back on the mantel*)

PETE   Maybe you better not forget those, huh?

TEMPLE   Go on!
(*He takes up the two packed bags and crosses to the door, passing* NANCY, *who is still looking at nothing and no one*)

PETE (*To* NANCY)   Not that I wouldn't like to, you know. For less than two thousand bucks even. For old lang syne. (*He transfers the bags to one hand, opens the door, starts to exit, pauses halfway out and looks back at* TEM-PLE) I'll be listening, in case you change your mind about the cigarette.
(*He goes on out, draws the door to after him. Just before it closes,* NANCY *speaks*)

NANCY   Maybe I was wrong to think that just hiding that money and diamonds was going to stop you. Maybe I ought to have give it to him yesterday as soon as I found where you had hid it. Then wouldn't nobody between here and Chicago or Texas seen anything of him but his dust.

TEMPLE   So you did steal it. And you saw what good that did, didn't you?

NANCY   If you can call it stealing, then so can I. Because wasn't but part of it yours to begin with. Just the diamonds was yours. Besides, he ain't even worried about whether or not you'll have any money at all when you get out to the car. He knows that all he's got to do is, just wait and keep his hand on you and maybe just mash hard enough with it, and you'll get another passel of money and diamonds too out of your husband or your pa. Only, this time he'll have his hand on you and you'll have a little trouble telling him it's— (TEMPLE *steps quickly forward and slaps* NANCY *across the face.* NANCY *steps back and throws the packet of money and diamonds to the floor.* TEMPLE *stops, looking down at the money and jewels.* NANCY *recovers*) Yes, there it is, that caused all the grief and ruin. If you hadn't been somebody that would have diamonds and a husband that you could find almost two thousand dollars in his britches pocket while he was asleep, that man wouldn't have tried to sell you them letters. Maybe if I hadn't taken and hid it, you

would have give it to him before you come to this, or
maybe if I was to take it out to where he's waiting in that
car right now, and say, Here, man, take your money—

TEMPLE   Try it. Pick it up and take it out to him, and see.
If you'll wait until I finish packing, you can even carry
the bag.

NANCY   I know. It ain't even the letters any more. Maybe
it never was. It was already there in whoever could
write the kind of letters that years afterward could still
make grief and ruin. The letters never did matter. You
could have got them back at any time; he even tried
to give them to you twice—

TEMPLE   How much spying have you been doing?

NANCY   All of it— You wouldn't even needed money and
diamonds to get them back. A woman don't need it. All
she needs is womanishness to get anything she wants from
men. You could have done that right here in the house,
without even tricking your husband into going off fishing.

TEMPLE   A perfect example of whore morality. But then,

if I can say whore, so can you, can't you? Maybe the
difference is, I decline to be one in my husband's house.

NANCY I ain't talking about your husband. I ain't even
talking about you. I'm talking about two little children.

TEMPLE So am I. Why else do you think I sent Bucky
on to his grandmother, except to get him out of a house
where the man he has been taught to call his father, may
at any moment decide to tell him he has none? As clever
a spy as you must surely have heard my husband—

NANCY (*Interrupts*) I've heard him. And I heard you
too. You fought back—that time. Not for yourself, but
for that little child. But now you have quit.

TEMPLE Quit?

NANCY Yes. You gave up. You gave up the child too.
Willing to risk never seeing him again maybe. (TEMPLE
doesn't answer) So that settles Bucky. Now answer me
this one. Who are you going to leave the other one with?

TEMPLE Leave her with? A six-months-old baby?

NANCY   That's right. Of course you can't leave her. Not
with nobody. You can't no more leave a six-months-old
baby with nobody while you run away from your husband
with another man, than you can take a six-months-old
baby with you on that trip. That's what I'm talking about.
So maybe you'll just leave it in there in that cradle; it'll
cry for a while, but it's too little to cry very loud and so
maybe won't nobody hear it and come meddling, especially with the house shut up and locked until Mr. Gowan
gets back next week, and probably by that time it will
have hushed—

TEMPLE   Are you really trying to make me hit you again?

NANCY   Or maybe taking her with you will be just as easy,
at least until the first time you write Mr. Gowan or your
pa for money and they don't send it as quick as your
new man thinks they ought to, and he throws you and the
baby both out. Then you can just drop it into a garbage
can and no more trouble to you or anybody, because then
you will be rid of both of them— (TEMPLE *makes a con-
vulsive movement, then catches herself*) Hit me. Light
you a cigarette too. I told you and him both I brought
my foot. Here it is. (*She raises her foot slightly*) I've
tried everything else; I reckon I can try that too.

74

TEMPLE (*Repressed, furious*) Hush. I tell you for the last time. Hush.

NANCY I've hushed. (*She doesn't move. She is not looking at* TEMPLE. *There is a slight change in her voice or manner, though we only realize later that she is not addressing* TEMPLE) I've tried. I've tried everything I know. You can see that.

TEMPLE Oh yes, nobody will dispute that you tried. You threatened me with my children, and even with my husband— You even stole my elopement money. Though at least you brought it back. Pick it up.

NANCY You said you don't need it.

TEMPLE I don't. Pick it up.

NANCY No more do I need it.

TEMPLE Pick it up, anyway. You can keep your next week's pay out of it when you give it back to Mr. Gowan. (NANCY *stoops and gathers up the money and the jewelry and puts them on the cocktail table.* TEMPLE, *quieter*)

Nancy. (NANCY *looks at her*) I'm sorry. Why do you force me to this—hitting and screaming at you, when you have always been so good to my children and me—my husband too—all of us—trying to hold us together in a household, a family, that anybody should have known all the time couldn't possibly hold together? even in decency, let alone happiness?

NANCY I reckon I'm ignorant. I don't know that yet. Besides, I ain't talking about any household or happiness neither—

TEMPLE (*With sharp command*) Nancy!

NANCY —I'm talking about two little children— Do you want them to know shame, like us?

TEMPLE I said, hush.

NANCY I can't hush. I'm going to ask you one more time. Are you going to do it?

TEMPLE Yes!

76

NANCY   You got to say it out in words yourself, so I can hear them. Say, I'm going to do it.

TEMPLE   You heard me. I'm going to do it.

NANCY   Money or no money.

TEMPLE   Money or no money.

NANCY   Children or no children. (TEMPLE *doesn't answer*) To leave one with a man that's willing to believe the child ain't got no father, willing to take the other one to a man that don't even want no children— (*They stare at one another*) If you can do it, you can say it.

TEMPLE   Yes! Children or no children! Now get out of here. Take your pay out of that money, and get out. (TEMPLE *goes quickly to the chair by the phone table and puts last-minute things into the open bag.* NANCY *crosses quietly toward the nursery, picking up a milk bottle from the table as she passes, and goes on*) What are you doing?

NANCY (*Still moving*)   This bottle has got cold. I'm going

77

to warm it in the bathroom. (*Then* NANCY *stops and looks back at* TEMPLE, *with something so strange in her look that* TEMPLE, *about to resume packing, pauses too, watching* NANCY. *When* NANCY *speaks, it is like the former speech: we don't realize until afterward what it signifies*) I tried everything I knowed. You can see that.

TEMPLE (*Peremptory, commanding*) Nancy.

NANCY (*Quietly*) I've hushed.
(*She exits through the door into the nursery.* TEMPLE *crosses to the seat in front of the fire, walks quickly to the cocktail table, picks up her handbag and sits, takes up the money and puts it in her handbag. Then she turns to the baby's bag, tidies it, checks rapidly over its contents and closes it. All this takes about two minutes; she has just closed the bag when* NANCY *emerges quietly from the nursery, without the milk bottle, and crosses toward the kitchen*)

TEMPLE Now what? (NANCY *goes on slowly toward the door.* TEMPLE *watches her*) Nancy. (NANCY *pauses, still not looking back*) Don't think too hard of me. (NANCY *waits, immobile, looking at nothing. When* TEMPLE *doesn't continue, she moves again toward the door*)

If—it ever comes up, I'll tell everybody you did your best. You tried. But you were right. It wasn't even the letters. It was me. (NANCY *moves on*) Good-bye, Nancy. You've got your key.

(NANCY *stops.* TEMPLE *shrugs. Now moving rapidly and with determination, she takes up the blanket from the table and crosses to the nursery door and exits through it. In another few seconds—perhaps four or five—*TEMPLE *backs out of the nursery—turns— sees* NANCY *standing still with her back to* TEMPLE. *She is now frantic—goes quickly to* NANCY *and, clutching both hands to her head, she screams—and as* NANCY *slowly walks away the bell begins to toll and the lights begin to dim, fading swiftly back toward complete darkness—as* TEMPLE *falls on the steps and the doors open to reveal the* GOVERNOR'S *office*)

Scene 3

GOVERNOR'S *office. 3:09* A.M. *March twelfth.*

The lights go on. The scene is the same as before, Scene 1, except that GOWAN STEVENS *now sits in the chair behind the desk where the* GOVERNOR *had been sitting and the* GOVERNOR *is no longer in the room.*

TEMPLE *does not know that the* GOVERNOR *has gone and that her husband is now in the room.*

TEMPLE (*Her face still hidden*)   And that's all. The police came, and Nancy still sitting in a chair in the kitchen in the dark, saying "Yes, Lord, I done it," and then in the cell at the jail still saying it—

> (STEVENS *leans and touches her arm, as if to help her up. She resists, though still not raising her head. She raises her face, quite blindly, tearless, still not looking toward the chair where she could see* GOWAN *instead of the* GOVERNOR, *into the full glare of the light*)

STEVENS   Get up, Temple.

> (*He starts to lift her again, but before he can do so, she raises herself, standing, her face still turned away from the desk, still blind; she puts her arm up almost in the gesture of a little girl about to cry, but instead*

*she merely shields her eyes from the light while her
pupils readjust*)

TEMPLE (*To* STEVENS) This time it certainly won't take
long, since all he has to say is, No. (*She still thinks the*
GOVERNOR *is sitting behind the desk*) Because he isn't
going to save her, is he? Because all this was not for the
sake of her soul, but for mine. So now you can tell us. It
won't be difficult. Just one word— (*She turns suddenly,
sees* GOWAN *sitting where she had thought all the time
that the* GOVERNOR *was sitting and listening to her. She
stops, arrested, utterly motionless, but even then she is
first to recover*) Oh God.

GOWAN (*He rises quickly*) Bitch.

TEMPLE (*She whirls to* STEVENS) Why is it you must
always believe in plants? Yes, Gowan was here first—
that was what you called that leaking valve, when we
stopped at the filling station to change the wheel, to let
him get ahead of us. (*To* GOWAN) I'm sorry, I was the
one that started us hiding things on each other, wasn't I?

GOWAN Maybe we both didn't start hiding soon enough—
Where are those letters? (*He has paused for an instant*)

I guess the guy will try to sell them to me direct this time. Which he may not do, since I won't swap him a lay for them.

(*He goes on around the desk, now heading toward where he entered*)

STEVENS   I have them.

TEMPLE   You have—
        (GOWAN *stops*)

STEVENS (*To* TEMPLE)   Nancy took the letters that night and gave them to me.
        (GOWAN *begins to laugh, harsh and bitter, mirthless. He turns to go*)

GOWAN   Not even a lay.

STEVENS   Where are you going?

GOWAN (*Walking*)   To get drunk—unless I have forgotten how in all these years. Or have you a suggestion?

STEVENS   What about Bucky?

GOWAN He's at your house with Maggie. Isn't that safe?
They don't murder babies there too, do they? (*He turns,
starts toward the right, from where* TEMPLE *and* STEVENS
entered, then stops) That's right. I'm probably still supposed to use the spy's entrance.

(*He turns back, starts around the desk again, and
exits*)

TEMPLE Oh God. Again. (*Not moving yet*) Tomorrow
and tomorrow—

STEVENS (*Speaking her thought, finishing the sentence*)
—he will wreck the car again against the wrong tree, in
the wrong place, and you will have to forgive him again,
until he can wreck the car again in the wrong place,
against the wrong tree— Come on. It's late.

TEMPLE (*Holds back*) Wait. The Governor said, No?

STEVENS Yes.

TEMPLE Did he say why?

STEVENS Yes. He can't.

TEMPLE   Can't? The Governor of a state, with all the legal power to pardon or at least reprieve, can't?

STEVENS   That's just law. If it was only law, I could have pled insanity for her at any time, without bringing you here at two o'clock in the morning— The Governor wasn't even talking about justice. He was talking about a child, a little boy—the same little boy to hold whose normal and natural home together, Nancy didn't hesitate to cast the last gambit she knew and had: her own debased and worthless life.

TEMPLE   Oh yes, I know. So good can come out of evil.

STEVENS   It not only can, it must.

TEMPLE   But I quit. Nancy told you that too.

STEVENS   She doesn't think so now. Isn't that what she's going to prove Friday morning?

TEMPLE   Friday. The black day. The day you never start on a journey.

STEVENS   Except that Nancy's journey didn't start at daylight or sunup. Her journey started that morning years ago when you got on that train—

TEMPLE   Oh God, that was Friday too; that baseball game was Friday—

STEVENS   You see? There is a corruption even in just looking at evil, even by accident. (*Gently tries to start her*) Come on.

TEMPLE   (*Holding back*)   Tell me exactly what he said. Not tonight: it couldn't have been tonight—

STEVENS   He said it a week ago—

TEMPLE   (*Wildly*)   So it was not even in hopes of saving her life, that I came here at two o'clock in the morning. It wasn't even to be told that he had already decided not to save her. It was not even to confess to my husband, but to do it in the hearing of two strangers, something which I had spent years trying to expiate so that my husband wouldn't have to know about it. Don't you see? That's just suffering. Not for anything: just suffering.

STEVENS You came here to affirm the very thing for which Nancy is going to die tomorrow morning: that little children, as long as they are little children, shall be intact, unanguished, untorn, unterrified.

TEMPLE (*Quietly*) All right. I have done that. Can we go home now?

STEVENS Yes.
 (*She turns, moves toward the right,* STEVENS *beside her. She falters, seems to stumble slightly, like a sleep-walker.* STEVENS *steadies her, but at once she frees her arm, and begins to speak*)

TEMPLE (*To no one, still with that sleepwalking air*) To save my soul—if I have a soul. If there is a God to save it—a God who wants it—

Curtain

86

ACT THREE

ACT THREE

Interior, the jail. 10:30 A.M. March twelfth.

Same set, stripped of furniture—just a long wooden bench stage center. The large gray louvered doors in the center are replaced by black doors with vertical jail bars. There are also jail doors downstage left and right, replacing the fireplace and the nursery door.

The door, left, opens with a heavy clashing of the steel. MR. TUBBS *enters.*

MR. TUBBS Come in, come in. (TEMPLE *enters from upstage left, followed by* STEVENS. TEMPLE *wears the same dress and coat.* STEVENS *is dressed exactly as he was in Act Two.* MR. TUBBS *is a typical small-town turnkey, in shirt sleeves and no necktie, carrying the heavy keys on a big iron ring against his leg as a farmer carries a lantern.* TEMPLE *stops just inside the room.* STEVENS *stops also.* MR. TUBBS *closes the door and locks it on the inside with another clash and clang of steel, and turns.* NANCY'S *voice can be heard, singing a hymn)* Well, Lawyer, singing school will be over after tonight, huh? (*To* TEMPLE) You been away, you see. You don't know about this, you ain't up with what's— (*He stops himself quickly; he is*

*about to commit what he would call a very bad impolite-
ness. He tries to rectify it*) Not that I wouldn't too, if I'd
a been the ma of the very— (*Stopping himself again;
this is getting worse than ever; now he not only is looking
at* STEVENS, *but actually addressing him*) Every Sunday
night, and every night since last Sunday except last night
—come to think of it, Lawyer, where was you last night?
We missed you— Lawyer here and Nancy have been
singing hymns in her cell. The first time, he just stood
out there on the sidewalk while she stood in that window
yonder. Which was all right, not doing no harm, just
singing church hymns. Because all of us home folks here
in Jefferson and Yoknapatawpha County both know Lawyer Stevens, even if some of us might have thought he
got a little out of line—(*Again it is getting out of hand;
he realizes it; but there is nothing he can do now; he is
like someone walking a foot-log; all he can do is move
as fast as he dares until he can reach solid ground or at
least pass another log to leap to*)—defending a nigger
murderer, let alone when it was his own niece was mur—
(*And reaches another log and leaps to it without stopping*)—maybe suppose some stranger say, some durn
Yankee tourist, happened to be passing through in a car,
when we get enough durn criticism from Yankees like
it is—besides, a white man standing out there in the cold,

while a durned nigger murderer is up here all warm and
comfortable; so it happened that me and Mrs. Tubbs
hadn't went to prayer meeting that night, so we invited
him to come in; and to tell the truth, we come to enjoy
it too. Because as soon as they found out there wasn't
going to be no objection to it, the other nigger prisoners
joined in too, and by the second or third Sunday night,
folks was stopping along the street to listen to them in-
stead of going to regular church. Of course, the other
niggers would just be in and out over Saturday and
Sunday night for fighting or gambling or drunk, so
just about the time they would begin to get in tune,
the whole choir would be a complete turnover. In fact,
I had a idea at one time to have the Marshal comb the
nigger dives and joints not for drunks and gamblers,
but basses and baritones. (*He starts to laugh, guffaws
once, then catches himself; he looks at* TEMPLE *with
something almost gentle, almost articulate, in his face*)
Excuse me, Mrs. Stevens. I talk too much. All I want
to say is, this whole county, not a man or woman in
the whole state of Mississippi, that don't—don't feel—
(*Stopping again, looking at* TEMPLE) There I am, still
at it, still talking too much. Wouldn't you like for Mrs.
Tubbs to bring you up a cup of coffee or maybe a Coca-
Cola?

TEMPLE   No, thank you, Mr. Tubbs. If we could just see Nancy—

MR. TUBBS   Sure, sure.

(*He disappears through the door on the right.* STEVENS *takes the same pack of cigarettes from his overcoat pocket, though* TEMPLE *has declined before he can offer them*)

TEMPLE   No, thanks. My hide's toughened now. I hardly feel it. People. They're really innately, inherently gentle and kind. That's what wrenches . . . something. Your entrails, maybe. The member of the mob who holds up the whole ceremony while he dislodges a family of bugs or lizards from the log he is about to put on the fire— (*There is a clash of another steel door offstage as* MR. TUBBS *unlocks* NANCY'S *cell.* TEMPLE *pauses, turns and listens, then continues rapidly*) And now I've got to say, "I forgive you, sister." No: it's worse: I've even got to turn it around. I've got to start off my new life being forgiven again. How can I say that? Tell me. How can I? (*She stops again and turns further as* NANCY *enters from the right cell, followed by* MR. TUBBS, *who passes* NANCY *and comes on*)

MR. TUBBS (*To* STEVENS) Okay, Lawyer. How much time
you want? Thirty minutes? an hour?

STEVENS Ten minutes should be enough.

MR. TUBBS Okay. Ten minutes, then.
(*He exits, closes the door and locks it behind him;
the lock clashes, his footsteps die away.* NANCY *has
slowed and stopped where* MR. TUBBS *passed her.
Her face is calm, unchanged. She is dressed exactly
as before*)

TEMPLE Nancy—
(*Almost at the same moment,* NANCY *herself speaks,
to* STEVENS, *so that it takes* TEMPLE *a fraction of a
second to catch on to what they are talking about*)

NANCY (*To* STEVENS) Did you give them to Mr. Gowan?
(*When* STEVENS *answers,* TEMPLE *is still that fraction of a second late, turning to him*)

STEVENS Yes. This morning. Just as you told me to.
(*Again* TEMPLE *is that fraction late, trying to catch
up*)

NANCY   Then I reckon they're burned up by now.

STEVENS   Yes.

TEMPLE   The letters? (*To* STEVENS) You have already given them to him? (*Wildly*) You lied to me. (*She begins to laugh, wildly and hysterically, striving for control*) Don't you see? It's all a waste? You lied to me when you didn't have to, you gave him the letters when he didn't even need them—it's all a waste, of lying and letters too.

STEVENS   (*Sharply*)   Temple.

NANCY   He ain't read them. He burned them.

TEMPLE   Gowan? Burned them?

NANCY   Maybe there was a heap of things he wasn't raised not to do, but reading other folks's letters ain't one of them, least of his wife's, to another man. He burned them up.

TEMPLE   Oh God, you're lying. You're going to die tomorrow morning, yet you're lying too.

94

STEVENS Hush. Listen.

NANCY (*In the same flat, level voice*) He can't quit now. If he had read them, maybe he could. But he burned them up, quick, so he wouldn't even have to not read them any more. Any quitting now, you'll have to do it.

TEMPLE Yes. All right. (*To* NANCY) I came back—

NANCY From California, they tell me. I used to think maybe I would get there too, some day. But I waited too late to get around to it.

TEMPLE So did I. Too late and too long, not only for you, but for me too.

NANCY And you come back, yesterday evening. I heard that too. And I know where you were last night, you and him both. (*Indicating* STEVENS) You went to see the Mayor.

TEMPLE Oh, God, the Mayor. No: the Governor, the Big Man himself. Of course; you knew that as soon as you realized that Mr. Gavin wouldn't be here last night to help you sing, didn't you? In fact, the only thing you can't know is what the Governor told us. No matter how clairvoyant you are, because we were not even talking about you; the reason I had to go and see him was not to beg or plead, but because it would be my right, my duty, my privilege— Don't look at me, Nancy.

NANCY   I'm not looking at you. Besides, it's all right. I know what the Governor told you. Maybe I could have told you last night what he would say, and saved you the trip. Maybe I ought to have—sent you the word as soon as I heard you were back home, and knowed what you and him—(*Again she indicates* STEVENS *with that barely discernible movement of her head, her hands still folded across her middle as though she still wore the absent apron*)—both would probably be up to. Only, I didn't.

TEMPLE   Why didn't you, Nancy?

NANCY   Because I went on hoping: the hardest thing of all to get rid of, let go of, the last thing of all poor sinning man will turn aloose. Maybe it's because that's all he's got. Leastways, he holds on to it, even with salvation already in his hand and all he needs is just to shut his fingers, old sin is still too strong for him, and sometimes before he even knows it, he has throwed salvation away just grabbling back at hoping. But it's all right.

STEVENS   You mean, when you have salvation, you don't have hope?

NANCY   You don't even need it. All you need, all you have to do, is just believe.

STEVENS   Believe what?

NANCY   Just believe. I know what the Big Man told you. And it's all right. I finished all that a long time back, that same day in the judge's court. No: before that even: in the nursery that night, before I even lifted my hand—

TEMPLE (*Convulsively*)   Hush. Hush.

NANCY   All right. I've hushed. Because it's all right. I can get low for Jesus too. I can get low for Him too.

TEMPLE   Hush! Hush! At least, don't blaspheme.

97

NANCY What's wrong with what I said? Jesus is a man too. He's got to be. Menfolks listens to somebody because of what he says. Women don't. They don't care what he said. They listens because of what he is.

TEMPLE Then let Him talk to me. I can get low for Him too, if that's all He wants. I'll do anything He wants if He'll just tell me what to do.

NANCY Trust in Him.

TEMPLE Trust in Him. Look what He has already done to me. Maybe I deserved it. But look what He did to you. Yet you can still say trust in Him. Why? Why?

NANCY I don't know. But you got to trust Him. Maybe that's your pay for the suffering.

STEVENS Whose suffering, and whose pay? Just each one's for his own?

NANCY Everybody's. All suffering. All poor sinning man's.

STEVENS   Then you believe that the salvation of the world is in man's suffering. Is that it?

NANCY   Yes, sir.

STEVENS   How?

NANCY   I don't know. Maybe when folks are suffering, they will be too busy to get into devilment, won't have time to worry and meddle one another.

TEMPLE   But why must it be suffering? Why couldn't He have invented something else? Or, if it's got to be suffering, why can't it be just your own? why can't you buy back your own sins with your own agony? Why do you and my little baby both have to suffer just because I decided to go to a baseball game? Do you have to suffer everybody else's anguish just to believe in God? What kind of God is it that has to blackmail His customers with the whole world's grief and ruin?

NANCY   He don't want you to suffer. He don't like suffering neither. But He can't help Himself. He's like a man that's got too many mules. All of a sudden one morning, he looks around and sees more mules than he can count at one time even, let alone find work for, and all he knows is that they are his, at least don't nobody else want to claim them, and that the pasture fence was still holding them last night where they can't harm themselves nor nobody else. And that when Monday morning comes, he can walk in there and hem some of them up. And that, once the gear is on them, they will do his work and do it good, only he's still got to be careful about getting too close to them, or forgetting that another one of them is behind him, even when he is feeding them. Even when it's Saturday noon again, and he is turning them back into the pasture, where even a mule can know it's got until Monday morning anyway to run free in mule sin and mule pleasure.

STEVENS   You have got to sin, too?

NANCY   You ain't *got* to. You can't help it. And He knows that. But you can suffer. And He knows that too. He don't tell you not to sin, He just asks you not to. And He don't tell you to suffer. But He gives you the chance. He gives you the best He can think of, that you are capable of doing. And He will save you.

STEVENS You too? A murderess? In heaven?

NANCY I can work. There's still the work to be done—
the washing and sweeping, maybe even the children to
be tended and fed and kept from harm and out from
under the grown folk's feet?

STEVENS Maybe even that baby?
(NANCY *doesn't move, stir, not looking at anything
apparently, her face still, bemused, expressionless*)

NANCY That one too. A heaven where that little child
will remember nothing of my hands but gentleness because now this earth will have been nothing but a dream
that didn't matter. Because I loved that baby, even at the
moment I raised my hand against it.

TEMPLE Is there a heaven, Nancy?

NANCY I don't know. I believes.

TEMPLE Believe what?

NANCY I don't know. But I believes.

*(They all pause at the sound of feet approaching be-
yond the exit door, all are looking at the door as the
key clashes again in the lock and the door swings
open and* MR. TUBBS *enters, drawing the door to behind him)*

MR. TUBBS (*Locking the door*) Ten minutes, Lawyer.
You named it, you know: not me.

STEVENS I'll come back later.

MR. TUBBS (*Turns and crosses toward them*) Provided you
don't put it off too late. What I mean, if you wait until
tonight to come back, you might have some company;
and if you put it off until tomorrow, you won't have no
client. (*To* NANCY) I found that preacher you want.
He'll be here about sundown, he said. He sounds like
he might even be another good baritone. And you can't
have too many, especially as after tonight you won't need
none, huh? No hard feelings, Nancy. You committed
about as horrible a crime as this county ever seen, but
you're fixing to pay the law for it, and if the child's own
mother—(*He falters, almost pauses, catches himself and
continues briskly, moving again*) There, talking too much
again. Come on, if Lawyer's through with you. You can

start taking your time at daylight tomorrow morning,
because you might have a long hard trip.
(*He passes her and goes briskly on toward the door.*
NANCY *turns to follow*)

TEMPLE (*Quickly*) Nancy. You're going to be all right,
but—(NANCY *doesn't pause.* TEMPLE *continues, rapidly*)
—what about me? Even if there is a heaven and somebody
waiting in it to forgive me, there's still tomorrow and
tomorrow. And suppose tomorrow and tomorrow, and
then nobody there, nobody waiting to forgive me—

NANCY (*Moving on after* MR. TUBBS) Believe.

TEMPLE Believe what, Nancy? Tell me.

NANCY Just believe.
(*She exits behind* MR. TUBBS. *The steel door offstage
clangs, the key clashes. Then* MR. TUBBS *reappears,
unlocks the door and opens it out again, pauses*)

MR. TUBBS Yes, sir. A long hard way. If I was ever fool
enough to commit a killing that would get my neck into
a noose, the last thing I would want to see would be a

preacher. I'd a heap rather believe there wasn't nothing after death than to risk the station where I was probably going to get off. (*He waits, holding the door, looking back at them.* TEMPLE *stands motionless until* STEVENS *touches her arm slightly. Then she moves, stumbles slightly and infinitesimally, so infinitesimally and so quickly recovered that* MR. TUBBS *has barely time to react to it, though he does so*) Here; you set down on the bench; I'll get you a glass of water. (*To* STEVENS) Durn it, Lawyer, why did you have to bring her—

TEMPLE (*Recovered*) I'm all right.

MR. TUBBS You sure?

TEMPLE Yes. (MR. TUBBS *passes on out the door and exits, invisible though still holding the door and waiting to lock it*) Anyone to save it. Anyone who wants it. If there is none, I'm sunk. We all are. Doomed . . . Damned . . . Finished.

STEVENS Of course we are. Hasn't He been telling us that for going on two thousand years?

MR. TUBBS (*Offstage: surprised*) Howdy, Gowan, your wife's in here.

GOWAN'S VOICE (*Offstage*) Temple.

TEMPLE Coming.
(*She looks at* GAVIN, *makes her decision, rises and moves toward the door. The curtain begins to fall as* TEMPLE *looks back through the bars at* NANCY'S *cell,* STEVENS *watching* TEMPLE)

Curtain